Santa Fe Trail

VOYAGE OF DISCOVERY
The Story Behind the Scenery ®

text
by
Dan Murphy

photography
by
Bruce Hucko

DAN MURPHY, during his career with the National Park Service, became fascinated with historic places, especially what you could learn from "being there" that wasn't in the books. He's followed the Santa Fe Trail in winter and summer, and by small plane. Murphy is also the author of *Lewis & Clark*, *John Wesley Powell*, and *Oregon Trail* in the "Voyage of Discovery" series.

BRUCE HUCKO, photographer and art educator, lives at Trail's end in Santa Fe. He travels the Southwest, making images and teaching children's art. Bruce especially appreciates the private landowners and buffs who keep the Trail alive!

Front cover: Army freight wagon, Fort Larned National Historic Site. Inside front cover: Point of Rocks, Cimarron National Grassland. Page 1: Detail of wagon brake. Pages 4/5: Iron sculptures near Council Grove, Kansas.

Edited by Mary L. Van Camp. Book design by K. C. DenDooven.

Second Printing, 1998

SANTA FE TRAIL, VOYAGE OF DISCOVERY: The Story Behind the Scenery. © 1994 KC PUBLICATIONS, INC.
*"The Story Behind the Scenery"; "in pictures... The Continuing Story"; the parallelogram forms
and colors within are registered in the U.S. Patent and Trademark Office.*
LC 94-75107. ISBN 0-88714-086-6.

Franklin, Missouri

Santa Fe

Santa Fe Trail
VOYAGE OF DISCOVERY

The trick was not just to cross the prairie between Kansas City and Santa Fe. Any competent frontiersman with a horse—and that meant any frontiersman—could do that. Francis X. Aubrey made himself a legend by doing it in two hours less than six days. The trick was to drag a *wagon* across that 900 miles of grass and storm. A horse could carry a man, but a wagon could carry enough to make a man rich. So the wagon would become the focus of the trip—to push, pull, cajole, repair, curse at, sleep under, modify into a boat, hide behind, sometimes finally to burn. But somehow the wagon and its straining animals had to get the cargo to the customers—who happened to be a third of a continent away. As it turned out, a wagon could carry ideas as well as textiles, and could change history. But a wagon could be a problem, too . . . and therein lies the story.

Sometimes geography and politics clash, sometimes they cooperate, but they cannot get a divorce. There was lots of geography, as well as time, between the Spanish Empire on the North American continent, and the rambunctious young country called the "United States." Spain got here first, at least from a European point of view and ignoring the Indians already old on the land. Columbus, an Italian, was sailing for Spain on his voyage of discovery in 1492.

Spain seized the opportunity and exploded into the New World. Within fifty years she had built one of the grand empires of world history, including not only vice-royalties on the newly discovered continents of North and South America, but on the rim of the newly defined Pacific Ocean as well. Mexico City rivaled or even surpassed Madrid, as did other colonial capitals. Important to our story, but not much noticed at the time, was the remote sub-colony that Spain threw northward from what we call Mexico today. Even then they called this remotest outpost of the empire "New Mexico," a name oddly gained before the revolution that would bring "old" Mexico into being.

New Mexico was a "bubble colony," not even on the edge of the mother culture, as some frontiers are. It was like a fishing lure thrown far into the pond, the rarely disturbed ruts of the *Camino Real* (Royal Highway—actually a wagon trail) the barest thousand-mile fish line of a connection back to Chihuahua City and Mexico City. For a while it had been a missionary colony, paid for by the crown, but after the great Pueblo Revolt of 1680 and the Reconquest in 1692, Spain had backed off on her religious and cultural goals for the Indians.

Mines had proved rare and poor, so even though the climate and soils were poor for farming, that's what it was—a poor, remote farming community. There was virtually no manufacturing. For any textiles, for tin and mirrors and books and weapons, annual wagon trains made an incredible trek across a thousand desert miles, back down to Chihuahua City.

Of course, the Chihuahua merchants "saw them coming" in every sense of the word, and prices were jacked sky-high. But the New Mexican colonists were trapped. Spanish law decreed that they must trade

"...Wagon after Wagon...Wagon after Wagon...Wagon after Wagon..."

Repeated throughout the account of Matt Field,
newspaper writer and editor who crossed the Trail in 1839.

with Spanish merchants and no one else. So they paid the price, pulled the carts and wagons back north to their remote homes, scratched what crops they could from the rocky soil, raised their kids and worshiped in primitive chapels—and from the point of view of a modern observer, enjoyed some of the best scenery on the continent. But that does not show up in the records.

Why did Spain bother to keep the colony? It certainly supplied no riches to the motherland, and in fact continually sent frantic messages for more settlers, more supplies, more help against raiding Indians. The answer lay not here, but in Europe and across the endless plains that lay east of New Mexico. Generations earlier Spain had been cock of the walk in the New World, but times had changed.

As the years of the 1700s wound by, France had risen to power, and England too, and both were challenging Spain's dominance in the New World. And they were just on the other side of those plains! (One guesses that many prayers arose from New Mexico chapels, thanking God for the endless stretches east from Pecos.) Here was the new value of the New Mexico colony. It was a buffer, the first line of defense of Spain's main holdings in middle America, especially the silver mining districts in the north, against competitors in North America.

Nor were England and France the only worries for Spain. In 1776 England's colonies on the eastern seaboard revolted and, to everyone's surprise, won. The new nation was called the United States of America. The baby nation did not seem like a real threat at first, but somehow this new form of government seemed to release the energies of its people in an almost frightening way, if you were a neighbor.

Fears multiplied in 1803 when France's Napoleon Bonaparte, short of cash for his European wars, sold the Louisiana Territory to the United States. Now this energetic, almost rambunctious young country with its ambitious entrepreneurs was almost next door. In fact, no one was even sure where the border was. Now the buffer colony was desperately important.

Spain tightened regulations against trade with non-Spanish merchants. The few who somehow crossed the prairies and showed up in Santa Fe had their goods confiscated and were jailed or sent south to Mexico City, often to be jailed there. An American army exploring party under Lt. Zebulon Pike wandered in—they claimed to be lost, but many think they were checking out the territory—and they were captured and sent south too. Later they were released, and Pike's report on the trade to be had in Santa Fe was widely published in the United States.

Politics was denying geography. The United States had goods Santa Fe wanted, and it was cheaper to haul goods across the plains than to import them to the port of Veracruz and up the immensely more difficult Camino Real to Santa Fe.

Spanish politics could hold that back for a while, but not forever. Already there were rumblings of revolution in New Spain, by people who wanted a new country to be called Mexico, and if that happened, surely they would change the policy. All this eventually would lead to that fabulous road of international commerce, drama and yes, even romance . . . the Santa Fe Trail.

The Trail was inevitable. Looking down from an imaginary historian's chair suspended somewhere high above Kansas, one sees a grand, 600-mile prairie, with busy little gatherings on two sides of it, like electrodes waiting for a spark to connect them. On the east were the settlements at the edge of the young United States. Here the loosest of the loose, or perhaps the most ambitious, already had pushed to the edge of the country and were looking westward. True, they'd read Pike's report of his crossing, and he'd labeled it the "Great American Desert," but for folks already on the frontier that wasn't too daunting.

Far on the other side were the villagers of Santa Fe, needing manufactured goods readily available in the United States. The settlers did not know it yet, but the God-view of the historian could see something else—there was no fatal barrier on that prairie. A man, more importantly a man with a wagon, could make it across if his gumption lasted as long as his ambition. And, already gathered at the edge, were men of "restless enterprise" willing to make the try. Invisibly, lines of commercial and personal energy aligned themselves across the prairie, waiting for the spark.

Where did the Santa Fe Trail begin? It began in the need of a Mexican farmer for manufactured goods; it began in the clear eye of a merchant seeing the opportunity for legitimate profit; it began in a government's change of policy. And, it's as good as anywhere to say it began in Franklin, Missouri, U.S.A.

"Then, hold your horses, Billy,
    Just hold them for a day;
I've crossed the River Jordan
        And I'm bound for Santa Fe."

"...a company of men destined to the westward.... Every man will fit himself for the trip with a horse, a good rifle, and as much ammunition as the company may think necessary for a tour or 3 month trip.... It shall be my business to apply to the governor for permission to proceed as far as we wish to go."

William Becknell in the Missouri Intelligencer, *June 25, 1821.*

It's doubtful that William Becknell had any idea what he was starting. He was a hard-bitten, hard-working frontier settler, one of the chips already carried west on the nation's tide. He'd been born in the Blue Ridge Mountains in Virginia when America was just a few years old. By 1810 the young man had drifted west to the frontier. There he fell in with the Boone brothers, sons of the famous Daniel Boone who had opened the westward trail across the Appalachians.

Money was scarce on the frontier. Once Becknell borrowed $321 and couldn't repay it—and that little fact changed the history of the United States. In debt and worried, Becknell opted to risk all on a venture that in those days could make you rich or dead. He decided to cross the dangerous, unknown prairies to trade with the Indians.

Becknell and a dozen or so others crossed the Missouri in the fall of 1821 and rode west. They found no Indians—some historians guess they actually weren't looking—and in mid-November the travel-ragged band rode into Santa Fe. There they found that instead of being jailed as foreign intruders, they were mobbed with customers for their meager goods. The revolution had come! With financial salvation in the form of silver coins packed in rawhide bags, Becknell

and his men hurried back to Franklin, taking a short-cut they'd guessed at across the eastern New Mexico plains. Importantly, Becknell realized that next time, a wagon could make it.

Rumor has it that back home he slashed the bags and the coins rattled onto the cobblestones. Historians doubt it, but the symbol is as useful as the fact. The road to Santa Fe was open.

Slightly salty water still flows from the spring at Boone's Lick, now a Missouri State Historical Park. Here the Boone brothers, and for a while William Becknell before he left for Santa Fe, had a business boiling the saline water to produce salt to sell to local settlers.

The old ferry crossing, where early Santa Fe Trail entrepreneurs crossed the Missouri River from Boone's Lick (the far side) to Arrow Rock, and headed west. Becknell and his small band crossed here in September 1821, on their historic trip which opened the Santa Fe Trail. After floods destroyed the original trailhead at Franklin, and river transportation improved, the trailhead kept moving west, leaving this abandoned crossing far behind.

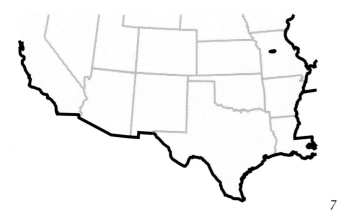

"...the great spring caravan to Santa Fe. A great number of our fellow citizens are getting ready to start.... We wish them a safe and profitable trip, a speedy return to their families and homes in health, and may they long live to enjoy the profits of their long and fatiguing journey of nearly one thousand miles, through prairies inhabited only by savages and wild beasts."

Fayette Intelligencer, *May 2, 1828.*

If William Becknell's Mexican coins ever did ring on the cobblestones, the bell started the damnedest wagon race there ever was. Up to now most of young America's commercial freight, and especially its long distance freight, had moved by river. But now the growing nation was bumping against the edge of the plains. A new class of merchants and entrepreneurs would have to learn the skills of massive, long distance wagon travel. And learn they would—and so would Mexican merchants, following the new road the other way.

Word of Becknell's trip spread quickly on the frontier "grapevine." By warm stoves in isolated country stores, at hitching posts by county courthouses, by firelight in remote cabins people talked of the fabulous profits to be had in Mexico. You just had to get there! Wagons were pulled from sheds and reconditioned as much as possible for a trip longer than any of them had ever taken. Cracked spokes had to be replaced, sideboards braced, grease buckets filled. Harnesses were oiled and spliced where necessary, and spares prepared.

These were not the great freight wagons of later years, when the trade would be taken over by highly capitalized companies. These were small groups of frontiersmen, grabbing the chance while it was hot and doing it with the best wagon they could lay their hands on. They counted their pennies, traded rumors about what might sell in Santa Fe, and made warmup trips that later would seem short back to St. Louis to buy goods.

Even before Becknell could get started on his second trip (when he used the wagons), his old neighbor Benjamin Cooper set out with two nephews and a trading party. They were successful. In 1824 a large party set out, led by a newcomer to the frontier, Col. Meredith M. Marmaduke. Marmaduke may have been a newcomer, but he was competent, proved by the fact that he thrived in the frontier's uncertain waters. In 1824, the same year he settled in Old Franklin, he led a group of 25 wagons of mixed vintage (carts, road wagons, and even Dearborn carriages) and some pack stock to Santa Fe, made his profit and got it back safely. Marmaduke could navigate political waters as well as the prairie—twenty years later he was elected governor of Missouri.

Precious springs would be the magnets that attracted travelers and determined campsites all along the Trail. This one, Santa Fe Spring in Arrow Rock, Missouri, the easternmost, carries in its common names the two-way nature of the trade—it was also known as Arrow Rock Spring.

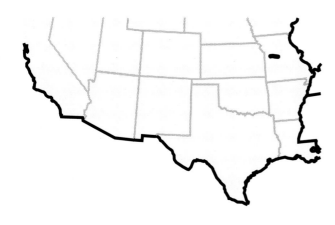

The Huston Tavern in Arrow Rock, Missouri, was built by William Huston about 1834. No log cabin, this substantial stone building (also called Arrow Rock Tavern) signified the permanence and substance the Santa Fe trade soon brought to the Missouri frontier. Many Santa Fe traders and travelers stayed here.

"The Missouri River is very low and the M. Star has much difficulty in getting
up...Grounded last night & made but little progress...grounded again in night and run
badly...About 1 Oclock ran aground on Balbirnam Bar—Sent passengers (gents) on
a sandbar where they remained until near dark. Got under way after dark...Arrived at
Kansas about 4 oclock P.M."

James Ross Larkin, 1856.

For the serious traveler in the 1800s, rivers were a contradiction. As long as a river was going your way it was a boon—a highway, long before highways were made of concrete. So great were the economies of moving a heavy load on water that even upstream travel was cheaper than using wagons. But if the river crossed your path, it was instantly a serious problem. Even pulling your wagon alongside a river had its problems. It meant you had to force your way across every tributary the river had. Not only that, but the closer you followed the river, the more you struck every tributary near its mouth, where it was deepest and widest and hardest to cross. It was a "Catch 22," and eventually it killed the river ports of Franklin, Arrow Rock, and even Independence.

Starting at St. Louis, the Gateway to the West for a century, the Missouri River, even upstream, was a help for more than 300 miles. For a while, including 1821, when Becknell left, the settlement of Franklin was about as far upstream as you could go. Steamboat technology at that time could not reliably breast the Missouri's current above there. So Becknell forced the crossings of the subsequent tributaries of the Missouri until its decisive turn to the north, and then headed on west overland.

But steamboat technology evolved—better valves, better gears, better hull designs—and by 1827 steamboats could push their way as far as the big turn of the Missouri at today's Kansas City (a meadow then). Meanwhile, the Missouri's inevitable floods had devastated the settlements of Booneville, Franklin, and Arrow Rock. So steamboats puffed their agonizingly slow way up to the new settlement of Independence, Missouri.

For decades, Independence would thrive as the trailhead of the Santa Fe Trail, but even that couldn't last forever. The landing at Independence had troublesome sandbars. Furthermore, after you off-loaded the wagons at Independence, you still had to cross the major Blue River, coming down to empty into the Missouri. It was geographically inevitable that in later years Westport, the westernmost landing on the Missouri before it swung north and out of the picture, became the final kickoff point for the overland drama of the Santa Fe Trail.

In any case, the beginning of the Santa Fe Trail was water. Would-be merchants bought goods and sometimes even wagons in St. Louis, then booked passage on a steamboat up the Missouri. They took the wheels off the wagons, then lashed the wagon boxes to the deck of the steamboat. There followed an uncertain number of days struggling against floating trees, sandbars, wind, and all the problems of an untamed river draining half a continent. Finally ashore, it was time to load the wagons for the longest trip they'd ever had.

As long as Independence, Missouri, was the trail head, Cave Spring, south of there, was a convenient noon stop on the first day for departing caravans. As some teamsters, at least, still were greenhorns, one wonders at the scenes that must have unfolded here, as caravans stopped for "nooning," then attempted to get animals and wagons moving again!

In the early 1900s the Daughters of the American Revolution did a remarkable job of marking the Santa Fe Trail with stone markers, still valuable and noteworthy today. This beginning marker is in Independence Square, Independence, Missouri.

"...enormous wagons into which men are packing bales and boxes. Presently the mules are driven in from pasture...catching the fractious animals...and introducing them to harness for their long journey.... The drivers snap their long whips and swear at their unruly mules, bidding goodby in parentheses between oaths, to old friends...."

Matt Field, 1839.

"Roll out! Roll out!" Legend says that this bellow from the wagon master got a wagon train moving, but the truth is there was a world of activity before that. A journey of a thousand miles to Santa Fe may have begun with a single step, but that first step was like that of a parachutist—a monster.

Risks had already been taken. The would-be trader had bought goods, then reconditioned the best farm wagons he could get. (In later years huge wagons were custom-made for the trade.) He needed a crew too, and that was not always easy. The footloose on the frontier may have come there by freedom-loving competence—or maybe they'd been misfits. He hired whomever he could.

On October 6, 1826, that indispensable chronicle of the frontier *The Missouri Intelligencer* published the following item:

"Notice is hereby given to all persons, that Christopher Carson, a boy about 16 years old, small of his age, but thick set; light hair, ran away from the subscriber living in Franklin, Howard county, Missouri, to whom he had been bound to learn the saddler's trade, on or about the first of September last. He is supposed to have made his way towards the upper part of the state. All persons are notified not to harbor, support or assist said boy under the penalty of the law. One cent reward will be given to any person who will bring back the said boy. David Workman."

Who would have hired a runaway apprentice with a disdainful one cent award on his head? Actually the bored young boy had hired onto a Santa Fe wagon train—and he became that ultimate frontiersman, Kit Carson.

The chaos of beginning. Greenhorn teamsters tried to break and harness greenhorn oxen or horses, while bemused oldsters puffed their pipes or called advice. Francis Parkman observed it for us, in Westport in 1846:

"The first step was an unfortunate one. No sooner were our animals put in harness than the shaft mule reared and plunged, burst ropes and straps, and nearly flung the cart into the Missouri. Finding her wholly uncontrollable, we exchanged her for another, for which we were furnished by our friend Mr. Boone of Westport, a grandson of Daniel Boone, the pioneer. This foretaste of prairie experience was very soon followed by another. Westport was scarcely out of sight when we encountered a deep muddy gully, of a species that afterward became but too familiar to us, and here for the space of an hour or more the cart stuck fast."

In later years the Santa Fe Trail became a stagecoach route as well, and the Mahaffie Stage Station at Olathe, Kansas, was a favorite stop just after the Civil War. Maintained today by the City of Olathe.

The Kansas City home of William Bent, one of the great names on the Santa Fe Trail. Bent and his older brother, Charles, made a fortune in Santa Fe and Indian trading, and built the imposing Bent's Fort on the Arkansas in the 1830s. In 1858 William purchased this house, perhaps as a second home. He died 11 years later at his ranch far west of here, near the old fort.

In spite of the confusion of starting out, it was a blessing that the first few days of travel were relatively easy—at least compared to what would come later. Geography supplied a break-in period. There was water and shade, and nearly always someone nearby who had been there or who knew the way and the techniques. True, today's traveler transported back then would find problems to write home about. But those were the problems any traveler back then was used to, in the civilized east as well as here beyond the frontier. How to keep warm, how to cure a sick horse, how to cross a stream, how to fix or jury-rig a wagon and tack, how to find food, and to find the way—problems exotic to us were as immediate and normal as we regard fixing a flat tire.

Along here the road from Fort Leavenworth came in. (They called them "roads" then, pavement not being necessary for that designation.) In early years there was no Fort Leavenworth. Later, after New Mexico became part of the United States (a gift of the Trail), army freight from the Fort became the major traffic on the Trail. A steady stream of the relatively small, tightly disciplined, efficient army wagon trains joined here, making their way to Fort Union, thence forts throughout the Southwest.

Josiah Gregg, an early trader and the great contemporary chronicler of the Trail, described the problems of the starting days. True, worrisome Indians did not come this far east, and there was plenty of water. But the necessary starting date was spring, when grass was green to feed the stock. That meant rain, troublesome in itself—and rain meant mud. To boot, the animals were not yet accustomed to the trek, often acting up at hitch-up time in the morning, or any other time the work required of them did not meet their fancy. "We had a foretaste of those protracted, drizzling spells of rain, which, at this season of the year, so much infest the frontier prairies. It began sprinkling about dark, and continued pouring without let or hindrance for forty-eight hours in succession...." Gregg recorded that he rolled himself in his blanket and crawled into a wagon, but he was lucky. Often fully loaded wagons meant teamsters slept outside.

And the mud! Do not imagine crossing the prairie as walking alongside a wagon on a sunny day. Rather, think of you and a friend trying to get a piano out of the basement, heaving step by step. "On such occasions it is quite common for a wagon to sink to the hubs in mud...to extricate each other's wagons we had frequently to employ double and triple teams, with 'all hands to the wheels' in addition—often led by the proprietors themselves up to the waist in mud and water."

Fantasies of easy riches at the end of the Santa Fe Trail dissolved quickly in the spring rains.

Originally Lone Elm campground, Olathe, Kansas, the first out of Westport, was a grove of trees, but within a few years most had been cut for firewood. By 1846, Susan Magoffin described the lone elm as the only one left, even though the grass was still high. Undoubtedly grazing by the draft animals soon reduced that as well.

When to leave was a critical decision. Santa Fe teamsters had to start after the grass had greened to "fuel" the animals, but still wanted to be ahead of most of their competitors. Usually they met the prairies as spring and summer flowers bloomed, such as this short-lived blossom of the spiderwort.

"Sunday Sept 25. Very fine morning. At 1/2 past 8 we started, but had scarcely gone 100 yds. before Capt. Brannin one of the Waggoners, broke his Waggon tongue short off. All hands were instantly Set to work to repair this mishap, Some getting Buffalo tugs [thongs], some splinters &c. & we succeeded in mending the tongue perfectly strong and secure, & were again under way at 5 M[inutes] past 10."

George Sibley, 1825.

Wagons in museums look old and weathered. It is easy to think they were old even when they were new, but how wrong that is! Even the color is misleading. Traditionally they were painted with blue bodies and red trim, with shining white Osnaburg canvas tops. A fresh caravan setting out was a "Fourth of July parade" of the most modern freight-hauling vehicles available!

Santa Fe wagons stood at the apex of wagon development. The heavy freight wagons which came to dominate the overland trade were triumphs of modern wagon engineering. The Trail saw every kind of wagon there was—ambulances for light fast travel, short wheelbases for tight mountain corners, special wagons for special loads—but most of all, the huge lumbering freight wagons. Do not disdain them from our exalted point of view in the 20th Century. They were the up-to-date Fruehoffs of their day.

Most prominent in our national memory is the "Conestoga," a European design with a rounded belly and raised ends, designed to cause a load to settle together on rough roads. The boatlike appearance gave rise to the phrase "Prairie Schooner," a vivid image crossing the seas of grass. It is hard to document actual Conestogas on the Trail, but the word came to be loosely applied to most heavy-duty freight wagons.

The earliest Santa Fe Trail wagons were whatever a farmer-turned-trader could fix up and manage to get all the way across the prairies. As the trade

boomed, wagonmakers emerged to meet the need. Wagon size increased as merchants calculated their transportation costs. This trend toward bigger wagons got a boost in 1839 when the Spanish Governor, Manuel Ármijo, decreed a $500 tax per wagon, regardless of how much the wagon hauled. Naturally the more you could haul in one wagon, the less tax there was per pound.

Builders in St. Louis, Independence, and even as far as Michigan (where a builder found a way to use prison workers, cutting his labor costs) designed and built huge wagons—some capable of carrying more than three tons. Designs evolved as well as size. In later years the boat-like Conestoga shape gave way to the more conventional box shape, probably because of ease of construction, particularly in larger numbers.

So the J. Murphy and the Eppenscheid wagon builders from St. Louis, the Schlutters from Michigan, the Studebakers from Indiana, took what they learned from the teamsters coming back from the prairies, and made the wagons that carried the cargo to Santa Fe.

"Conestoga" became a generic term for heavy freight wagons, including those used on the Santa Fe Trail, though most were not actually Conestogas. Trail-weary and weathered when seen in museums now, as here in the army museum at Fort Leavenworth, usually Santa Fe freight wagons were brilliant red, white, and blue when they started their journey!

The brake was engaged by lever-and-rod from the driver's bench, or from a position walking alongside. On steep downhill grades it could be assisted by dragging logs behind the wagon, or chaining the wheels to prevent their turning.

"It is now about 6 o'clock P.M. we are still in the same track. The wagons have started on and most of them are out of sight. The hindermost one has stuck in a mud hole and they are doubling and tripling teams to pull it out, and I believe have finally succeeded and now we will proceed."

Susan Magoffin, 1846.

They hauled their freshly packed wagons west, through the lovely, rolling hills of eastern Kansas. The wheels cut into the prairie sod, beginning the ruts that would fascinate us a century and more later. Once there is a rut, water runs down it, which keeps eroding the rut. So today, on a spring morning, you and I can walk in the footsteps of our forebears.

In most cases it is not so simple as the ruts showing us "the trail," the single spot where the wagons went. A wagon went where it was best to go—ten feet that direction, ten feet the other direction. Imagine yourself pushing a loaded wheelbarrow across the back yard. You'd tend to follow the least slope, even if it was longer. If it was muddy you'd avoid the puddle—if not, go straight across it. Santa Fe Trail teamsters had the added problems of grass for their animals to graze, and the need for firewood. A campsite that was ideal if you were the first wagon train that year, might be useless if you were later in the season. The firewood had been used, and the grass had been grazed. So you swung a mile north . . . and made a new rut.

Still, in some places geography came into play. Early teamsters all knew of "The Narrows" in this early stretch of the Trail, right after the Blackjack ruts. Here the drainage of the Wakarusa River to the north, and a stream called the Marais de Cygnes to the south forced wagon trains onto the ridge in between. If it was wet weather, common in spring when you hit this place, you had one choice—mud. Worse, in this restricted spot one stuck wagon could hold up an entire caravan. Often it was "all hands to the wheels."

In the middle years of the Santa Fe Trail, somewhere along here (the exact location changed over the years) the famous Oregon Trail of the pioneers branched to the north to seek its own destiny. Up to now the professional teamsters of the Santa Fe cargo trade had had a continual amusement of the amateur travelers alongside them, the pioneer families making the only transcontinental trip of their lives and determined to walk clear to Oregon and California.

You had to admire them, even if they did not have the expertise of many crossings. And they had *women* along, which quite changed the nature of a crossing. Now their farm wagons moved off to the north, the drivers remembering what they could of the advice they'd received from the seasoned Santa Fe teamsters—who enjoyed providing it. The professionals' freight wagons rolled on to the Southwest.

Ruts such as the "Blackjack Ruts," maintained by Douglas County, Kansas (near Baldwin City), are the most poignant, vivid remnants of the Santa Fe Trail. It is a rule of geology that linear scars tend to perpetuate themselves—in other words, ruts are a place for rainwater to run like a little stream, so they tend to keep eroding and perpetuate themselves. Thus it is possible a century later to contemplate genuine ruts made by Santa Fe Trail wagons.

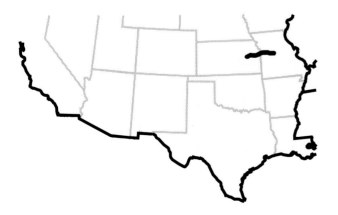

The Daughters of the American Revolution marker in Baldwin City, Kansas. These important markers were placed in the early years of this century (this one in 1907). The Trail was still a fresh memory then, so the DAR markers are valuable to scholars today. We owe thanks to the many dedicated individuals who donated labor, money, and research to place and to maintain them.

*"**B**oss, the trouble with them oxens is that they don't understand the kind of language we're talkin' to 'em. Plain 'Gee' and 'Haw' ain't enough under the present circumstances. Now, if you could just find it convenient to go off on that hill, somewhere, so's you couldn't hear what was goin' on, I'd undertake to get them oxens out."*

A teamster's comment to shipping firm owner William Waddell.

All observers commented on the characters drawn to the trade. From novices to scarred veterans, from profane mule skinners to those who quoted Virgil, the profession seemed to attract the unique and the curious—and to keep the competent.

A nation formed of immigrants showed it in the merchant bands she sent out. James Larken wrote in 1856, "In our train we have quite a number of nations represented—Americans, Mexicans, French, Germans & Pawnee Indians—numbering about 16 men." A train's teamsters were divided into "messes," usually ten or so in each, which cooked and ate as a group. One observer wrote that his mess had four Germans, two Irishmen, two Americans (whatever that meant), a Mexican, and an Englishman. One Irishman had been a wine bottler, the other a deserter from the army who was a singer and storyteller. Another in the group was "Woodpecker," enjoyed for his singing at the campfire. Examples could multiply infinitely. Surely they represented one of the most motley, remarkable groups in our country's history.

And they were competent—at least those who lasted. Of that there was no doubt, for they had a hard job to do, and there was no half-way. You either got the cargo to Santa Fe against awesome obstacles, or you didn't.

Generals have stars—the bullwhacker had his whip, his *panache*. This was no carnival whip we see today. It was a monster, suitable to driving oxen or

mules dragging three tons up the slope of the prairie to the Rocky Mountains. In the days of the professionals the whip started with a three or four foot stock of heavy wood, and then a braided rawhide lash that could be twenty feet long. On the end was a replaceable "popper," an eight inch piece of rawhide that could crack like a pistol shot, and could cut hide like a knife. But that was not the point of it. A teamster bragged if he could get to Santa Fe and back without drawing blood.

The point was to "pop" it at just the right spot, by the correct animal's left or right ear, to guide and inspire him. Of course this led to the showing off that comes down to us in carnivals, popping a friend's cigar, popping the head off a rattlesnake at twenty paces (it's said that rattlesnakes did not exist along the Trail in just a few years, victims of this sport), or popping a coin off a loosely driven stake without knocking over the stake.

No wonder that small boys in frontier towns, seeing these awesome men (who were not diminished in their own telling) leave in the spring, to reappear months later with tales of foreign and exotic places, grew up wanting to join them. Later, one remembered his school days on the frontier: "Oh! to be a bullwhacker! It meant so much! Think of it! Across the plains and back, camping all the way!"

Another roadside business to service Trail travelers in later years was the McGee-Harris Stage Station, Osage County, Kansas, built by Fry McGee, Oregon Trail veteran, about 1854. McGee also built a nearby toll bridge, and charged 25 cents per wagon.

After U.S. mail contracts made it feasible, the Trail was a stagecoach route as well. The stage trip from Independence to Santa Fe took 25 to 30 days in the 1850s, and amenities were sorely lacking. At best, a meal was a fast stop at a hostel such as this—the Simmons Point Stage Station, Douglas County, Kansas. Often one ate on the fly—or didn't.

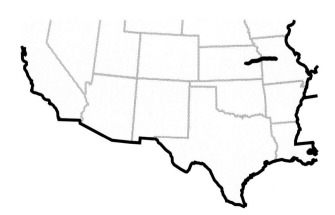

"...arrived to Breakfact at a Main Branch of The Nee Ozho River; and here we find most excellent pasturage, and a Large & beautiful Grove of fine Timber; and we determine to wait here for the Osages, who are expected in two or three days. Our Camp is arranged with the view of receiving our expected Visitors in a suitable manner. Very few flies Here."

George Sibley, August 5, 1825.

Council Grove got its name in 1825, the third year of the Santa Fe Trail. Already merchants on the frontier saw the potential of the trade, and of course so did politicians. Senator Thomas Hart Benton of Missouri thundered in his inimitable way to Congress that the road was the westward future of the nation, and got a bill passed that included $30,000 for a survey of the route. (This was trickier than it seems, as half of it was over foreign land.) George Sibley, an experienced frontiersman and Indian trading post factor (manager), was in charge.

The survey itself was not of much use—by now traders knew the way and could find it without the dirt piles the survey party made to mark the route. But what was important was that along the way they made treaties with Indian tribes to allow passage (for a price) of the wagon trains. The first and most successful treaty was arrived at under these oaks, with the Osage Indians. Sibley named it Council Grove.

Council Grove was a critical point on the Trail. Some even called it the beginning of the Trail. Up to here you had been within the frontier, but here you crossed it. From the Missouri River to here the Indians had been friendly, and so had the countryside, providing plenty of water, graze, and timber. But past Council Grove came the vast, open prairie. Past here streams would be far between, firewood rare, and the Indians often hostile.

So traders enjoyed the lush campsite and the clear running Neosho River, beautiful yet today. They cut heavy branches of hardwood, for none grew on the prairie beyond here, to sling under the wagons and carry for spare axles and tongues. (Iron axles were not introduced until 1845.) A teamster counted himself lucky if he could carry the extra weight clear to Santa Fe and back, *without* using it.

In early years merchants often traveled this far separately, a few wagons in a group. But here, facing the prairie, they organized into caravans and elected captains. This was important because someone had to make decisions about routes and campsites, and organize defense of the wagon train should the need arise. Given the outrageous individuality of the teamsters involved, that the system worked at all is credit to the restraint and good sense of those involved.

Two years after Sibley's council, Seth Hays, grandson of Daniel Boone, settled at Council Grove, and the town began. Through Trail days it thrived as a final fitting-out point for prairie travel. Its water and shade would be remembered at many a hot, dry, or dangerous camp far out on the way to Santa Fe.

Some wondrous stories are true. "Hermit's Cave" in Council Grove, Kansas, was one of several caves stayed in by Geovanni Maria Augustini, a mystic, reportedly the son of an Italian nobleman. In 1863, he walked with a wagon train from here to Las Vegas, New Mexico, where he stayed in another cave on what is now called "Hermit's Peak," where he is said to have done miracles. Later he was killed in southern New Mexico.

Council Grove, Kansas, was named when George Sibley, surveying the road to Santa Fe in 1825, held a council with the Osage Indians (the first of several such councils) negotiating right-of-way across the prairies. Tradition says that a particular huge stump, now preserved by the town, may be "the" oak. Whether that detail is true or not, this grove was important as the "jumping-off place" for the trek across the prairies.

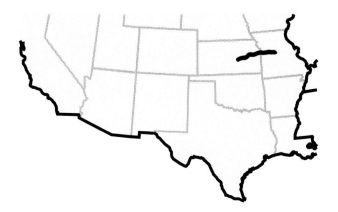

There's a story that appears over and over in the journals of the Trail. When the wagon trains first encountered buffalo, the novices and even some old-timers went wild. Veteran woodsmen from back East, who'd routinely hunted deer for sustenance on their farms, would fire empty guns, pack in a second ball before they'd fired the first, throw their ramrods away, and when there was nothing else left to do, ride pell-mell into the middle of the thundering horde and dash along, screaming. It was an unparalleled adrenalin rush. And when the herd drew away and the thunder faded, sometimes the hunter found himself far from the wagons or anything even familiar. For some it was just a few hours to find their way back—some never made it.

Sam Arnold, who owns the "Old Fort" restaurant near Denver and specializes in frontier cooking, has scoured old journals for recipes, and swears he's even tried them. Some startle the modern palate. Seventeen-year-old Lewis Garrand on his first trip wrote, "the men ate the liver raw, with a slight dash of gall by way of zest." Others seasoned it with raw marrow, or even gunpowder. (Garrand grew to like it "pretty well.") Another delight was "boudins." This was intestine, tied at the ends to prevent the escape of the partially digested grass (one needs his vegetables!), lightly seared and then laid on a saddle blanket, "looking for all the world like a dead snake," for all the hungry to attack.

Strips of buffalo meat cut thin and dried, often called "jerky," was an important survival item, being almost infinitely storable and providing tremendous nutrition. Don't judge it by the imitation displayed near check-out counters today. It was good stuff.

Bone marrow itself was a delicacy, which this author has tried and liked, and "fleece," the linear strips of meat along the top of the vertebrae, just may be one of the best meats man ever tasted, and that includes anything available today.

So they entered onto the prairie, bound for a foreign land and already seeing, experiencing, and even tasting the utterly new. Sitting by the fire one starry night, heart still pounding from "the chase" that afternoon, at some subconscious level they began to know that dragging these wagons to Santa Fe was not just another dry business investment. It just might be something about life as well.

Buffalo! The scientist today says technically they are "bison," but to Santa Fe Trail teamsters and pioneers who saw them in the thousands they were "Ol' buff." By any name they were a fascinating and exciting part of the prairie scene. As the Indians had for centuries, early teamsters often depended on them for food.

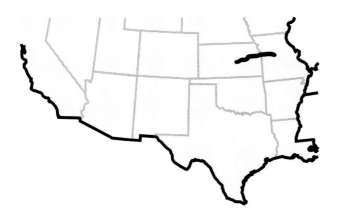

Spectacular Santa Fe Trail ruts near Durham, Kansas. Now the wagons were rolling onto the prairies, and as their wheels cut through the highly specialized root systems of prairie grasses, they created a stream bed for water and a playground for winds. Over decades ruts became swales, sometimes lasting to this day—to the delight of Santa Fe Trail buffs.

"...their wretched victim was taken off a few rods and shot down in cold blood. After his murder a considerable amount of gold was found about his person, and in his trunk. The body of the unfortunate man, together with his wagon and baggage was thrown into a neighboring ravine...their booty was packed...and borne away to the frontier of Missouri."

Report of Josiah Gregg, 1831.

Now we must explode one of the myths of the Santa Fe Trail. Long presented by Anglo schoolbooks as sharp Yankees going down to trade with the Mexicans, actual records reveal that at least by 1843, there were as many sharp Mexicans coming East to trade with the "Mericans" as there were Yankees going the other way. The murder of one of these Mexican merchants set off an uproar in the trade.

Prominent Mexican trader Don Jose Antonio Chavez set out from Santa Fe in 1843. Waiting on the prairie was a Missouri ne'er-do-well named John McDaniel, and his gang. McDaniel, who imagined himself a representative of the new republic of Texas, somehow thought attacking a wagon train would help Texas' feeble claim to New Mexico territory. Or maybe he just wanted to rob somebody. In either case, it was the Chavez train that came along.

The train already was in trouble. Having left Santa Fe too early, they'd hit a blizzard which had killed almost all 55 mules, and forced most of the men to return to Mexico. Some time back, at Pawnee Rock, Chavez had sent ahead a rider to seek help on the Missouri frontier. It is likely McDaniel intercepted this rider, and learned of Chavez' whereabouts. Now, just west of the Little Arkansas near Cow Creek, they met. The court testimony that would follow is contradictory, but the bottom line is Chavez was robbed and murdered, and his body dropped into Owl Creek. (Today, Owl Creek is Jarvis Creek—an Anglo mispronunciation of "Chavez.")

Another eastbound party, that of Nicholas Gentry, had been following Chavez' tracks and became suspicious when they turned off the Trail at Cow Creek, where they shouldn't have. After Gentry reached Missouri and learned Chavez had not arrived, he was on total alert. Gentry boarded a steamboat, and (this is almost a television plot!) suspicious-looking men boarded the steamboat to continue toward St. Louis. It was, in fact, McDaniel, but something tipped him off and he jumped ship. His accomplices were arrested. In panic they threw something overboard, and when it was recovered from the Missouri's waters it was discovered to be Mexican gold pieces. McDaniel himself was soon picked up.

At his trial McDaniel raised international questions, such as his being an agent of Texas sovereignty and not a mere thief. It didn't work, and on August 16, 1845, he was hung near the old Arsenal in St. Louis. The results were not minor. A subsequent Texas raid, led by Col. Jacob Snively, was put in disrepute and they ended up straggling home. And more importantly, Mexico and the United States began to solidify as trading partners, less as opponents.

Cow Creek Crossing, Kansas, was one of the bad ones. Stream beds were always a major problem on the Santa Fe Trail. The modern traveler little notices how much earth moving and paving has been done to produce the road he travels so easily at high speed.

Today the vegetation is dense here at the crossing of the Little Arkansas River in Kansas, but in Trail days a lone cottonwood signaled teamsters still distant on the prairie as to where they could cross this stream. Near here occurred one of the famous crimes of the Trail, the murder and robbery by Texas renegades of Mexican trader Jose Antonio Chavez. It was to have international repercussions.

> *"...Pawnee Rock...I was anxious to see this wonderful curiosity. We went up and while mi alma with his gun and pistols kept watch, for the wily Indian may always be apprehended here, it is a good lurking place and they are ever ready to fall upon any unfortunate trader behind his company—and it is necessary to be careful...I cut my name among the many hundreds inscribed on the rock...."*
>
> *Susan Magoffin, July 4, 1846.*

As the heavily loaded caravans toiled up the broad valley of the Arkansas, they were in Indian country. When encounters with the proprietors of the land they were passing through began to sour, politicians back home howled for military escorts for the wagon trains, and in 1829 one came along.

The army's budget was tight, and Major Bennett Riley did not have enough money even to buy mules for the wagons his 180 men would ride in, so he had to make do with oxen. This greatly amused the freighters he was supposed to be protecting, but unexpectedly the slow, steady oxen did as well over the long haul as horses or mules, and soon traders quit laughing and began using them too. (For the life of the Trail the relative value of mules and oxen was good fodder for argument, with personal preference usually deciding it.)

Riley's men escorted that caravan of 38 wagons all the way up the Arkansas Valley, with no incidents, then watched from the American side as the freighters crossed the river and headed into Mexican territory. Within days they were attacked by Indians. A rider came galloping back with the news. Riley risked an international incident by rushing onto Mexican territory, but he did relieve the siege of the wagon train. The Mexicans, of course, were as concerned about the safety of the trade as the Americans, and when that wagon train returned from Santa Fe it had a Mexican escort back to the Arkansas, where Riley had been waiting and picked it up again. There were incidents all along the way, but the cargo made it there, and the profits made it back.

One of the lessons learned (besides the value of oxen) was that a heavily armed wagon train, if it was well organized and knew what it was doing, was its own best protection. Until the massive outbreaks of Indian raids after the War with Mexico, traders mostly took care of themselves. Indians were always there, sometimes resentful of the trespassers and always interested in the riches packed in the wagons, but could not stop the trade, nor even slow it very much. Caution was no match for ambition.

Ash Creek Crossing, a few miles west of Pawnee Rock. Even when dry this could be a difficult crossing, with a steep east bank. Susan Magoffin's wagon upset here and she was knocked unconscious, the incident often blamed for her miscarriage later on the journey.

In Trail days Pawnee Rock was an important landmark, but much of it has been quarried in modern times for railroad and home construction. This was the heart of Indian country and many encounters took place near here. The rock also became a trail register as many, like Susan Magoffin, carved their names on it, but nearly all have been removed by quarrying.

"The Indians let out a war-whoop that warned us what we were to expect and came after us at redoubled speed. Their ponies stretched forward in a sweeping gallop and bullets and arrows began to sing about our ears. It would have been certain death for us to stop to fight, for the Indians hopelessly outnumbered us. It became now a race for life and our one hope was to keep ahead until they saw the soldiers coming...."

Charles Christy, 1867.

There was an idea for a while that the plains could remain "Indian country," with traders just passing through to get to Mexico. That wistful dream withered quickly. The heavily loaded wagons were too rich for the Indians to ignore, and the rich land they were crossing was too much for traders to ignore.

In 1846, an American army marched down the Santa Fe Trail and the War with Mexico opened, which we'll tell about later. It ended with America acquiring the north part of Mexico—and all hell broke out on the prairies. With America actively trying to "take over" the prairies, the Indians got serious about resistance. In 1847 alone the traders' losses totaled 330 wagons, 6,500 animals, and 47 dead traders and teamsters—and that's from incomplete records.

Now responsible for the whole Trail, the army began building forts at strategic points. Fort Leavenworth already anchored the eastern end of the Trail, and in 1851 Fort Union was planted at the west end. One of the most important in between was Fort Larned, in the heart of Indian country, built in 1858. In the next decade Fort Larned saw more Indian fighting than most forts saw in their lifetime. In one famous incident, the Kiowa Chief Satanta captured the fort's *remuda*, or horse herd, then sent word that they were poor horses and the army should provide him with better!

During the Civil War most of the army was pulled back east to fight Confederates, and the Indian Wars intensified. Harassed, undermanned Fort Larned escorted all the Santa Fe trade caravans it could, even while it launched various expeditions to take the war to the Indians. Incongruously, in between screaming engagements it served as the area agency, distributing goods decreed by treaty to the various tribes. It was one of the Fort Larned-based military campaigns, that of George Custer in 1868 (who became immortal by proving the mortality of himself and his entire 7th Cavalry a few years later), that largely reduced the Indian attacks on the Trail.

In the 1870s, the railroad that would end the Trail came through. Soldiers from Fort Larned protected that operation, and their job was finished. The fort, deactivated in 1878, is today a splendid national historic site.

Awesome blizzards can sweep the plains of Kansas, as Santa Fe Trail travelers sometimes learned the hard way. "Same night had a severe snow storm, which continued for 48 hours with such violence we were unable to keep a fire. Snow 3 feet deep, we were all more or less frozen," wrote Mexican trader Manuel Alvarez in 1842. He lost two men and forty animals on that crossing. (The ruts shown here are west of Dodge City.)

Throughout the 1860s Fort Larned, Kansas, was a center of U.S./Indian relations. Military expeditions from here protected the Santa Fe Trail and engaged in operations against the Indians during uprisings, but the fort was also an Indian agency in times of peace.

Overleaf: Bent's Old Fort with replica of a Conestoga wagon at the front gate.

"It having been determined upon, however, to strike across this dreaded desert the following morning, the whole party was busy in preparing for the 'water-scrape,' as these droughty drives are very appropriately called by prairie travellers...the captain's voice is usually heard above the din and clatter of the camp, ordering to 'fill up the water kegs'...."

Josiah Gregg, 1831.

Decision point. There were two routes from here to Santa Fe. Apparently Becknell himself, on his pioneer trip, kept following the Arkansas into present-day Colorado, then found his way over craggy Raton Pass and down the front range of the Rockies, to the gap where he could slip across to Santa Fe. Of course he soon figured out that he could cross the Arkansas River here and take a shortcut, cutting southwest toward New Mexico. It was shorter—but dry. And therein lay the rub. It was sand hillocks south of here, a terrible, dry haul to the Cimarron River. And would you find the Cimarron? Sometimes you went by compass like a ship on the sea, until ruts were clear. And when you got there, one watercourse looked like another, usually dry.

Still, traders liked the cutoff. The hundred miles saved might be a week's jump on the competition, and the dollars might be worth the risk. But then Kearney's Army of the West, marching down the Trail to conquer New Mexico (and California) in 1846, elected to continue up the Mountain Branch. They improved it some as they went, particularly the hard part at Raton Pass. That, plus the fact that Indian raids began exploding about then, almost closed the Cimarron Cutoff, and shifted most of the traffic to the Mountain Branch.

For the first years, fording the Arkansas here to force the desert on the other side was politics as well as geography, for the other side was Mexico. After Kearney and the War with Mexico, the politics made it all American—but the geography, the hard crossing and the sand hills, remained.

To start with, traders never did find a good crossing, because there wasn't one. Quicksand and holes bogged and tipped wagons and soaked cargo. The complex harness that hitched the animals to the heavy loads could break, or just as bad, tangle. Teams were unhitched and rehitched to double- and triple-up on the wagons, then crossed back to do it again. Then, while cargo dried in the sun, men filled everything that would hold water, even boots on at least one trip. Cooks prepared food for a couple of days, men and animals took final drinks they'd remember. Then, often in the evening to cross as much as possible in the cool night, they heaved on the wheels and started through the deep sand, leaving the Arkansas behind.

"Middle Crossing" of the Arkansas River, west of Dodge City, Kansas. A critical point on the Santa Fe Trail, this is where traders had to make the decision whether to ford the Arkansas River and risk the dry, but hundred miles shorter, Cimarron Cutoff into New Mexico; or to continue up the river on the longer, but in many ways safer, Mountain Route.

Today the "Cimarron Crossing" of the Arkansas River often is dry, its waters diverted for high plains irrigation. In Trail days it could be a perilous ford. Wagons often encountered quicksand as well as moving water.

Here is a branching. The next few pages will follow the Cimarron Cutoff of the Trail, before returning (on page 47) to follow the Mountain Route instead.

"The forlorn band were at last reduced to...cutting off the ears of their mules, in the vain hope of assuaging their burning thirst with the hot blood...a buffalo, with stomach distended with water, [was] discovered.... The hapless intruder was immediately dispatched, and an invigorating draught procured from its stomach. I have since heard one of the parties...declare that nothing ever passed his lips which gave him such exquisite delight as his first draught of that filthy beverage."

Second Becknell trip, 1822 (related by Josiah Gregg).

Not only was the Cimarron Desert hard, it came when men, animals and wagons were weary. The long haul up the prairie had worn them out. Parts already thrice-repaired broke again, even harder to fix again. The wood of wagon beds and parts shrank in the dry air. As the wooden wheels shrank the iron rims loosened or even came off. Back at the Arkansas they'd put the wheels in the water overnight to soak the wood and thus tighten the rims. But when they came off out here, you did the best you could with shims and wedges.

Indian raids were common on the Cimarron. It was their land, they knew how to survive on it, and besides the pride you could gain in defeating these intruders, there were those unimaginable goods to be had in the wagons! This is where the group Riley had been escorting ran into trouble, and Charles Bent himself had to wait until Riley could rush in to rescue him. This is where Josiah Gregg on one frightening occasion encountered a group of Indians he estimated at two or three thousand—fortunately it was a moving village with women and children, and not inclined to attack him.

But Indians or not, the desert would take its toll. Marian Russell in 1852 saw the same mirages others did here: "...a will 'o the wisp that beckoned and taunted. Sometimes it would look like a party of mounted Indians and the women would cry and begin counting their children. Sometimes it would look like a tall castle set among the trees, or a blue lake with waves lapping white sand. It danced ever before us...."

There was another illusion, one noted by the Spanish *conquistador* Coronado who had ventured onto these same plains some three centuries before. The sweep of the land made it seem as though the land gently sloped upward all around you. In the long afternoon you were an insect, slowly inching across the bottom of a vast bowl that moved along with you, meeting at the horizon the inverted bowl of the sky. Thirsty, weary, sometimes they dozed even as they walked, to jerk awake at the mirage of Indians coming over the rise. Men rested on wagon tongues, sometimes falling asleep to the wagon's monotonous, continual creaking, to fall over and be run over by the wagon—a surprisingly common accident. The Cimarron was no picnic.

By now wagons were showing the strain of the endless haul across the plains, rising to the Rocky Mountains which were yet to come. Repairs were needed almost daily, often ingeniously done with what was at hand. These hand-forged ox chains were unearthed south of Ingalls, Kansas, on the Cimarron Cutoff.

Santa Fe Trail ruts south of Ingalls, Kansas. Now they were on the infamous "water-scrape," pushing to the Cimarron River before man, beast, or wagon gave out. Stories abound of the hardships along here, nature's challenges multiplied by the common encounter with hostile Indians (who, it should be noted, apparently lived well in this area that traders found so difficult to cross).

"Here was one calling for balls—another for powder—a third for flints. Exclamations, such as 'I've broke my ramrod'—'I've split my caps'—'I've rammed down a ball without powder'—'my gun is choked, give me yours'—were heard from different quarters, while a timorous 'greenhorn' would cry out, 'Here, take my gun, you can outshoot me!'"

Josiah Gregg, 1831.

Today it is difficult to visualize the Cimarron Cutoff the traders saw. The modern traveler encounters well-kept farms and villages, drawing on the water of the great Ogallalah Aquifer.

It was desert when Jedediah Smith crossed it in 1831. There probably is a lesson in this, whether expertise in one field can be transferred to another. "Jed" Smith was one of the great ones, a "thirty-second degree mountain man" as Bernard DeVoto called him. The map of the American West was in his head, as were most of the tips on how to survive in it—but not all of them. He'd crossed South Pass when it was new, might have found Jackson's Hole, found the valley called Yosemite, and explored up the Pacific Coast and back again. Finally realizing that it was the companies, not the individual trappers, that were going to make the money, he and partners bought out William Ashley's American Fur Company and Smith made a respectable, though small, fortune.

Jed decided to sink that capital into the burgeoning Santa Fe trade. It was a fatal mistake. On his first crossing, he decided to take the shortcut across the Cimarron Desert. Why would that frighten the man who'd survived the terrifying desolation west of Great Salt Lake? With his old buddy "Broken Hand" Fitzpatrick (another 32nd degree) they crossed the Arkansas on August 23rd, 1831. August is hot. Within

days the party was desperate for water. They scattered out, and Smith, as so many times before, ventured on alone.

Somewhere around the Cimarron (the exact spot can never be known), he encountered Comanches. One story says he had his head down, drinking at the water hole he'd been desperately searching for. Others say the Comanches approached while he was still on his horse, and scared it by waving blankets so he was thrown off and temporarily helpless. At any rate, he killed one of them ("the chief," but that may be a story) and then they got him. Smith, the opener of much of the American West, died alone on the Santa Fe Trail, trying to learn a new trade. "Comancheros," Mexicans who made a specialty of trading with the Comanches, heard the story from the Indians, which is how it comes to you today. The Santa Fe trade always was a risky business.

Sometimes, if one was lucky, the Cimarron had water when the wagon trains got there. Even if not, if you recognized it you could dig down and find some, running just a few feet beneath the sandy surface. You rested and refilled, and had merely the rest of the Cutoff to face.

Middle Spring on the Cimarron River was a reliable source of water on a sometimes-dry river. Near here the legendary mountain man, Jedediah Smith, died on his first Santa Fe Trail crossing in 1831.

Traders sometimes called today's Cimarron National Grassland (managed by the U.S. Forest Service) the "sea of grass," visually apt save that it was dry. Navigation often was by compass. Teamsters were looking for the Cimarron River, but as it was dry as often as not, some crossed without even realizing it. At best the jornada *could be done in an all-night and all-day drive; for most it was several days. For some it took the rest of their lives.*

*"**F**rightening thunder storms came up suddenly.... When the sky would darken and the forked lightning sent the thunder rolling, the drivers would wheel the wagons so that the mules' backs were to the storm. The prairie would darken and then would come a mighty clap of thunder and a sheet of drenching water would fall from the skies upon us. A fine white mist would come through the tightened canvas.... So we would sit through wind, water, thunder, and lightning."*

Marian Russell, 1852.

In its day the Santa Fe Trail was often called the "road" to Santa Fe, for in some ways the existing roads back East—which were dirt too, after all—were not much better. Still, some problems were endemic to the prairie.

Storms, for instance. A half-dozen spectacular ones were par for any crossing, and they could cause problems a dozen ways. The torrent itself—and make no mistake, "desert" storms can be torrents—was merely an inconvenience. There was a rush to make sure the precious cargo was covered, that no canvas had come loose and would let rain wreck the merchandise this trip was all about. Already they'd spent precious hours day after day drying it out after river crossings. It was money lost to have to do it once again. And during the torrent, there was the deafening thunder and lightning that stampeded stock—another delay and cost.

Mostly the people just got wet, just like back in Pennsylvania. But here the problems did not stop when the rains moved past, to catch the wagon train behind them. Now it was mud. Men heaved on the spokes, inching the great wheels that turned grudgingly to drag the tons of wagon and cargo ahead. Until the ground dried it was hell on men and animals, but there was no choice.

Streams flooded too. If you came to a stream in the evening it was best to cross it then, rather than wait for morning. It might have rained upstream, and by morning it might be too deep to cross and you'd lose a day (and dollars). Besides, animals worn from the day's work were a little easier to manage in the evening, especially for a tricky stream crossing, than in the frisky morning.

Then there were prairie fires. For centuries the Indians had set them, noting the fine spurt of fresh grass that always followed a blaze. Lightning-starts were even more common. A big fire could be too far across for a wagon to escape. Your best bet was a counter-blaze, to use up fuel, if the wind allowed it, or getting to a creek bottom and toughing it out. But you didn't need to be near a fire to suffer from it. A burned area might take days to cross. There was nothing for the animals to eat. Worse, the charred stems cut animals' mouths. Luckily, prairie fires tended to burn in a patchwork. By hard pulling and luck one might still find some grass, if the fire itself had not eaten the precious wagon.

As travelers everywhere, those on the Trail could not resist a chance to leave their name on a handy rock. Autograph Rock on the Cimarron Cutoff, Oklahoma, became a favorite "register."

Point of Rocks was a Santa Fe Trail landmark on the Cimarron Cutoff, Kansas. The Santa Fe Trail was a merchant road, of people carefully calculating exchange rates and paying attention to the profit/loss column. Nevertheless there seems to have been an almost mystical element to the experience. Merchants who knew how to sharpen a pencil later told stories to their grandchildren about the journey—not about profit.

"One night a great thunderstorm came up. I had never known the wind to blow so hard .... I hid my head under Richard's arm and did not hear Colonel Carson calling. Richard was trying to find his clothing when the Colonel's cry changed suddenly into a roar of rage. His tent had fallen down upon him. Richard had to call out the Corporal of the guards to get the Colonel extricated."

Young bride Marian Russell at Camp Nichols, 1865.
(The colonel so outraged when his tent fell upon him was "Kit" Carson.)

Short-lived Fort Nichols on the Cimarron Cutoff did not participate in famous deeds, save the one described above. It is from the diary of Marian Russell, illuminated for us by historian Marc Simmon in *The Enchanted Land*, a favorite book of every Trail buff. Marian had come across the Trail in 1852 at age seven. Eventually she married one of Carson's officers, which led to the quoted incident.

One early, much more serious incident influenced the Cimarron Cutoff for decades. In the fall of 1828, a wagon train was returning from Santa Fe. Two young men, riding barely ahead of the train, got to a stream crossing and lay down to sleep in the autumn sun. For some unknown reason the unwatchful men were shot by Indians "with their own guns," shortly before the train came up. Young McNees was killed and Dan Munroe mortally wounded. The outraged teamsters carried the corpse and the survivor to the Cimarron River, where Munroe died.

As Gregg heard the story, just as the teamsters finished burying the two victims some Indians rode up. It seems certain the Indians had had nothing to do with the killings, or they would not have casually ridden up to the train. But with dirt from the graves still hanging on the shovels, the teamsters did not see it that way. They pulled their rifles and killed all but one of the approaching Indians. That one, of course, rode back to his people with word of the outrage. That put the fat in the fire.

The Indians put on their paint even as the train pushed across the Cimarron Desert, and attacked at the crossing of the Arkansas. Gregg says they got "nearly a thousand" of the teamsters' stock, some undoubtedly the profit of their trip. They then attacked another train, which probably had no idea of what had gone on.

(This latter battle may or may not have resulted in the famous "caches" near today's Dodge City, where traders are rumored to have buried a great amount of goods when their livestock was stolen, to come back and recover later.)

When unknown Indians killed a young teamster here at McNees Crossing, multiplied retributions by both sides bloodied the Cimarron Cutoff for decades.

Rocky, and jolting—Turkey Creek Crossing on the Cimarron Cutoff was an "easy" crossing. Now the wagons were crawling across the vast, dry plains of northeastern New Mexico, endless vistas punctuated by isolated volcanic uplifts.

McNees Crossing on the North Canadian River, New Mexico, is known locally as "Corrumpa Creek"—and as "Louse Creek" (for unknown but guessed-at reasons!) in some Trail journals.

"...altogether eleven dead bodies have been found; their persons have not been identified.... A party of citizens going hence to the States discovered the dead bodies...in such a state of decay as to show they had been killed ten or twelve days previous. The mail bags were broken open and the contents much scattered...."

Official report of U.S. Army Col. John Munroe, May 19, 1850.

Wagon Mound was a prominent landmark of the Trail, just as today it is an unmistakable sight on Interstate 25. Not only did it rise at the end of a long prairie crossing, useful as a marker, but it happened to look like a wagon and its teams—surely a sign!

It is hard to pinpoint the first shot of this ricochet of reprisal. A year earlier, in 1849, a group of Jicarilla Apaches camped near the growing town of Las Vegas, south of Wagon Mound. Already there had been incidents with details now lost, but the result was that young Lt. Ambrose Burnside (who would become famous some years later in the Civil War) was assigned to arrest the Jicarilla camp. It turned into a fight, with "many" Jicarilla killed. Apparently one of the prisoners taken was the daughter of the Jicarilla Chief Lobo.

Shortly thereafter, and almost certainly as a result, the Apaches attacked a wagon train near Wagon Mound and captured two white girls, and a month later, a few miles further out on the Trail, captured the wife of trader James White.

Now another ricochet. A troop of soldiers sent out after the White incident took Lobo's captured daughter as guide. Near Wagon Mound, she tried to escape or at least to kill soldiers or their mules, and was shot. More "incidents" followed—though they were more than incidents to the people, white and red, who died in them.

The ricocheting shell exploded in early May, 1850. A westbound U.S. mail wagon arrived at Wagon Mound. It may have been under a running attack already, the record is unclear. What is certain is that on May 19 a wagon train heading out on the Trail found the remains of the mail wagon and its party scattered about the hollow where the cemetery for the little town of Wagon Mound is today. Mail and papers blew about in the wind, scattered around the bodies of the eleven men who had accompanied the mail wagon.

A detachment summoned from Las Vegas gathered all the mail they could find, and buried the bodies in a mass grave. They burned the remains of the wagon over the grave, a common trail practice to hide graves from Indians or wild animals.

Mounting tensions on both sides surely hurried the creation of Fort Union, just a few miles closer to Santa Fe, the next year. The Cimarron Cutoff was showing—and causing—the conflicts that would virtually close it, as most traders began switching to the Mountain Branch of the Trail.

Traders saw the distinctive outline of Wagon Mound—a famous Trail landmark in New Mexico (actually the remains of an eroded lava flow), as a wagon with its weary teams—within a week or so of Santa Fe, and the end of the journey.

A remarkable gift from nature, this easy crossing—the Rock Crossing of the Canadian River, New Mexico—is almost on the natural route of the Trail, while just upstream the river becomes virtually uncrossable because of bottomless sand, and immediately downstream it enters a spectacular gorge.

This is almost the end of the Cimarron Cutoff. Now this narrative returns to the Arkansas River in Kansas, to follow the alternative Mountain Route to rejoin this route at Fort Union (just ahead).

> *"...the outside exactly fills my idea of an ancient castle...who could have supposed such a thing, they have a regularly established billiard room! They have a regular race track.... There is the greatest possible noise in the patio. The shoeing of horses, neighing, and braying of mules, the crying of children, the scolding and fighting of men, are all enough to turn my head."*
>
> *Susan Magoffin, 1846.*

Bent's Old Fort, that remarkable castle on the Arkansas. Likely the talents of the Bent brothers would have distinguished them in any era, but on the frontier they were a corporate and political force. Charles and William Bent had Indian trade in mind when they built the fort in 1833, but when circumstances brought the Santa Fe Trail by, the fort was ready. Here was commerce brought to the heart of the prairie. Men who met at this wilderness dining table were aware of prices in Madrid and London as well as in St. Louis, and talked about who to contact to effect legislation in Washington and Mexico City. Often huge bands of Indians, particularly Cheyennes (to whom William was related by marriage), camped outside and traded.

For many travelers, such as the bride Susan Magoffin who visited here in 1846, it was a touch of civilization after weeks of rugged travel. Tragedy touched young Susan here, as she experienced and recovered from a miscarriage brought on by the rigors of the Trail. At the same time Susan was experiencing her private grief, the whole U.S. Army of the West was resting and repairing, getting ready for the push into New Mexico.

Such was the brothers' standing that when New Mexico became a territory, Charles was appointed interim governor. Charles was killed in an uprising in Taos in 1847, and at about the same time the rising Indian wars killed the trade on the prairies. William destroyed the old fort that had been a symbol for so long. He established another, some miles downriver, but the grand days never returned.

The Bent brothers' establishment was not an army fort but a private establishment for trading with Indians, and resupply on the Santa Fe Trail.

Bent's Old Fort was one of the great reliefs of the Santa Fe Trail, recalled with affection by many weary travelers for the rest and repairs received there.

Often large bands of Indians gathered at Bent's Old Fort to trade—the owner, William Bent, was married to a Cheyenne lady. This National Park Service reconstruction at LaJunta, Colorado, gives visitors one of the best possible impressions of a frontier fort.

The trader who chose to skip the Cimarron Cutoff, but rather continued up the Arkansas River following the Mountain Route, found this the next major stop after the parting of the ways.

"We have been rather unfortunate today—a wagon was turned over this morning, and the bed and bows so much broken as to cause a delay of some hours to repair it sufficiently to travel on...almost every fifty or an hundred yards there are large stones, or steep little hillocks, just the things to bounce a wagon 'wheels up'...."

Susan Magoffin, 1846.

The Mountain Branch of the Trail suffered less Indian problems than the Cimarron Cutoff, less worry from Confederates during the Civil War, and you usually did not have to worry about finding water for the men or the stock. But there was one big headache—7,834 feet big to be exact. That was Raton Pass. It was a hard, steep pull, and then a downhill grade even more dangerous for wagons—if less exhausting. And these were wagons that already had crossed the prairie, and were showing the battering. Diaries record discarded parts scattered along the trail, each one a delay or a disaster for someone.

In 1866, the pass became the kingdom and story-telling domain of Richens Lacy Wooton, one of the remarkable characters the frontier seemed to produce on call. He'd been mountain man and rancher, wandering all over the Colorado-New Mexico area. Once he drove a herd of sheep over the Trail to Kansas City and exchanged them for milk cows, which he drove back to Pueblo, Colorado. He tried raising buffalo—that didn't work and he ended up selling the herd to a zoo in New York City. He operated a saloon and store in one frontier crossroads, but couldn't see a future in it and sold out. The place was called Denver.

Then "Uncle Dick" saw another opportunity—he would make a decent road through Raton Pass and charge people to use it. In 1865, he secured a charter from the Colorado legislature and went to work. No road by modern standards, nevertheless it was a great

improvement over the twisted trail that had taken its toll on wagons before that. Now it was Uncle Dick who collected the toll. He was a storyteller, and people remembered their encounters with him, or the nights they spent at the hostelry he built along with his ranch in the pass.

In the 1870s, as the railroad came west erasing the Santa Fe Trail, there was a race on Raton Pass. By coincidence the advance construction engineers of two competing railroads, the Denver and Rio Grande and the Atchison, Topeka and Santa Fe, approached Raton Pass on the same day, February 26, 1878.

While the D&RG's man stopped to grab a night's sleep, J.A. McMurtrie for the Santa Fe hired a horse, picked his way up the pass in the dark and woke up Uncle Dick. The deal he was offered looked good—he saw that the railroad would kill his business any way—$50 a month for life, payable in goods from the railroad's stores. The well-rested D&RG engineer arrived the next morning to find temporary workmen (they'd been travelers sleeping at the inn) scratching out the right-of-way. The Santa Fe became the railroad that opened the Southwest.

Trail merchant John Hough built his house in Trinidad, Colorado, about 1870, and subsequently sold it to western merchant Felipe Baca. Today it is managed by the Colorado State Historical Society.

This silent fragment hardly does justice to the rollicking history of the Clifton House, near Raton, New Mexico. Rancher Tom Stockton built it in the late 1860s, and soon it attracted stagecoaches using the Santa Fe Trail. Here travelers ate the "best food in northern New Mexico," teams were changed, business was transacted. The hotel boomed in the last years of the Trail...and died when the Trail did.

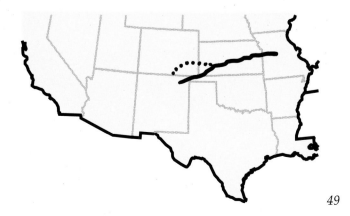

"At Fort Union our great cavalcade rested. The tired mules were turned out to graze on the prairies. Freight was unloaded and the two hundred horses turned into the corral.... The parade ground was a shambles of bales of buffalo hides, Mexican blankets and sheep pelts, things to be sent out on the out-going east bound train...."

Marian Russell, 1852.

Fort Union showed that the old Santa Fe Trail had come of age; in fact, the fort had a major hand in making that happen. No longer was the trade just a few annual caravans. When the U.S. took over New Mexico it established a whole series of forts throughout the West, and those forts had to be supplied. Now large civilian freighting companies developed, with government contracts to haul the mountains of material needed by the army and civilians as well, in the developing West. One giant firm, Russell, Majors & Waddell, could put as many as 350 wagons on the road at a time (and for a while, operated the short-lived Pony Express on the side.)

Most of this came into Fort Union. The sound of forges was constant background in the repair and wheelwright shops, while a small army of clerks kept track of what was going where over the network of roads developing in New Mexico. The hospital was the first one the injured and sick of the Trail came to—records show that disease took many, many more lives than Indian action ever did. The chapel was a touch of home (Marian Russell was married there). Even the jail found plenty of use, taking care of a different sort of Trail problem.

At the fort, or near it if there was no need to stop, the Cimarron Cutoff and the Mountain Branch came back together. And it was old Fort Union that superintended the continual improvement of the road from there to Santa Fe.

Fort Union was the largest wagon repair and rebuilding facility in the West—and anyone who'd just crossed the Trail knew why.

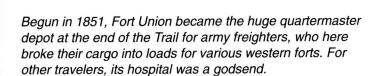

Begun in 1851, Fort Union became the huge quartermaster depot at the end of the Trail for army freighters, who here broke their cargo into loads for various western forts. For other travelers, its hospital was a godsend.

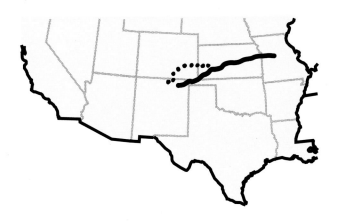

View from maintenance yard to the officers' quarters, Fort Union, New Mexico.

"The general pointed to the top of one of their houses...from that point, where all could hear and see, he would speak to them...`I have come among you by the orders of my government, to take possession of your country, and extend over it the laws of the United States...those who remain peaceably at home...shall be protected by me...But Listen! He who is found in arms against me, I will hang!'"

Lt. William H. Emory's report of U.S. Gen. Stephen Watts Kearney's proclamation in the plaza at Las Vegas, New Mexico, August 15, 1846.

Wagons could haul textiles and tools, books and booze and oysters, pianos and printing presses, and indeed they did haul all of those. But wagons brought *ideas* as well—ideas about food and clothing, about society, even political ideas. Soon Americans rented houses in Santa Fe, and Mexican merchants opened lines of credit in New York and enrolled daughters in finishing schools in St. Louis.

Coincidentally, when the revolution in 1821 brought Mexico into being, the new country had its own start-up problems and paid less attention to its Santa Fe colony. All this was watched by Mexican and American merchants alike. "Manifest Destiny" was never clearly defined, but the phrase had power. So did all those intertwined business interests. And in 1846 they loaded Manifest Destiny, whatever it was, into wagons at Fort Leavenworth and told Col. Stephen Watts Kearney to take them to Santa Fe.

The Army of the West marched out the Trail the summer of 1846, paused a while at Bent's Old Fort which had never seen such a crowd, then picked and axed their way over Raton Pass. They camped at a water hole near where Fort Union would be built a half-decade later, and finally came to the growing town of Las Vegas, the first outlier of Santa Fe.

They weren't quite sure what to expect from General (also Governor) Armijo and the Mexican Army, though they sent ahead well-connected merchants to try to smooth the way. And here in Las Vegas, General Kearney (his general's papers had caught up with him while the army was paused at Bent's Old Fort) climbed up on the roof of a store by the plaza, and announced that the annexation was happening.

It was not bloodless, as too many history books say. True, the first uncertain fall and winter were remarkably peaceful, but the next spring Charles Bent would die in an uprising in Taos, and many more would die before the transition was complete. But the Santa Fe Trail had done something probably few saw at the outset. It had tied New Mexico to the United States with merchant contracts, making it only a matter of time before politics caught up.

Starvation Peak, between Las Vegas and Santa Fe, was a prominent and unmistakable landmark of the Trail. Unfortunately, the romantic legends of starvation by persons—lovers, or pioneers, or what-have-you—marooned at the peak are undocumented. Similar stories appear at most striking peaks.

It was probably from the building in the center of the historic plaza in Las Vegas (now an excellent western bookstore), that General Stephen Watts Kearney, having just brought the Army of the West across the Santa Fe Trail, made his proclamation of occupation in 1846 during the U.S. occupation of New Mexico.

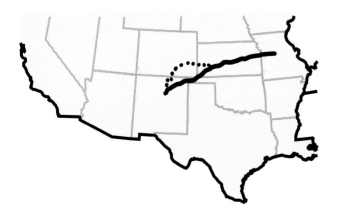

> *"...We entered San Miguel, the first settlement of any note upon our route. This consisted of irregular clusters of mud-wall huts, and is situated in the fertile valley of Rio Pecos, a silvery little river which ripples from the snowy mountains of Santa Fe—from which city this frontier village is nearly fifty miles to the southeast."*
>
> *Josiah Gregg, 1831.*

Whether early or late in the life of the Santa Fe Trail, San Miguel meant you were getting close. On Becknell's first trip he'd been brought to San Miguel first, though because of language difficulties did not learn about the Mexican Revolution and his welcome mat until he entered Santa Fe. For years it was the first settlement traders reached, or the last as they departed Santa Fe going east. For a while the Mexican government put the customs house in San Miguel, though it appears most of the actual transactions took place in Santa Fe.

During the time that the government put a $500 tax on each wagon, regardless of weight, some very over-loaded wagons came into San Miguel. Teamsters had realized they could cross the prairies with standard loads, then stop while still out on the plains, transfer the loads to as few wagons as possible, burn the empty wagons (worth a good deal less than $500 by now), and strain on into San Miguel. The sight of these burned remnants later may have led to estimations of even more Indian problems than there actually were.

After Las Vegas was founded San Miguel lost its "absolute frontier" status, but was still an important stop. As Kearney and the Army of the West came through, his officers and men were on edge, wondering just where they would run into the Mexican Army. As it turned out they never did, but coming in they'd been ready.

In 1841, the Republic of Texas sent an invasion force—or maybe it was a merchant expedition, no one could quite tell—toward Santa Fe. It came up the Pecos River intending to intersect the Santa Fe Trail here. Mexican President Santa Anna (yes, the same one) ordered New Mexican Governor Armijo to stop the invasion, if that's what it was. Near here Armijo did so, disarming the force and sending it back to Texas.

And then the whole area was American. Now wagon train after wagon train passed by, and troops and contractors showed up to work on the road, moving rocks and improving fords. The railroad and the interstate were still to come, and they would bypass San Miguel to cross the Pecos a few miles upstream; but this little town witnessed an amazing parade.

"Vado" means ford, and as the Pecos was sometimes a considerable stream the fords along this stretch upstream from San Miguel del Vado were important. This was the last major stream crossing before Santa Fe.

Until the founding of Las Vegas in 1835, San Miguel was the "outpost" of Santa Fe, the first Mexican village one encountered after the crossing. The Church of San Miguel del Vado was built in 1805. The bell was cast in Ohio in 1861, and must itself have been hauled over the Trail in a wagon.

> *"Even so late as ten years ago...the traveller would oftentimes perceive but a solitary Indian, a woman, or a child, standing here and there like so many statues upon the roofs of their houses, with their eyes fixed on the eastern horizon...while at other times not a soul was to be seen in any direction, and the sepuchral silence of the place was disturbed by the occasional barking of a dog...."*
>
> *Josiah Gregg, describing Pecos Pueblo, 1844.*

Sometimes cultures meet. Sometimes they collide. Here at Pecos they did both.

It was a meeting place for East and West long before the Santa Fe Trail epitomized that meeting. Pecos was of the Pueblo culture, the prehistoric farming culture that thrived in and near the valley of the Rio Grande. Pecos was the easternmost outpost of the pueblos, so to Pecos came traders from the plains before any wheels marked the way, bringing buffalo hides and other plains goods to exchange for the agricultural products of the Rio Grande. Pecos residents became trader specialists, the Pueblos who knew the language and ways of the plains people.

When the Spaniards came up from the south like a thunderclap, they soon found Pecos because it was in the gateway of travel to the plains. Expedition after expedition stopped here, sometimes to visit, sometimes to fight. The Pecos people now saw a culture and its products unlike anything they'd ever imagined. And the religion these newcomers had was new too, and the newcomers took it very, very seriously. Soon there was a mission here, and for centuries Pueblos heard about European faith. They were adaptable, and chose such parts of it as suited them, resisting others. But this enforced grafting of the two cultures did not work very well. Pecos waned as the Spanish population grew in this gateway village.

By the time the wagons began rolling through in the 1820s, Pecos was down to less than a hundred people, holding on in buildings that once held two thousand. This is the time Gregg described in the quotation above. After just a few years of Trail travel, the remaining handful of Pecos people abandoned the pueblo and walked through Glorieta Pass and past Santa Fe, to join their linguistic cousins at Jemez Pueblo, where they live today.

As for the abandoned village, Santa Fe Trail travelers continued to make the short side trip to visit the ruins and pick up odd souvenirs. From local old-timers they'd hear and relate the wondrous stories, by now wildly exaggerated, of the wondrous perpetual fire and the great snake of Pueblo mythology.

Pecos and its ruins in this critical pass have watched a centuries-long parade. Plains Indians came through, then Spaniards, and eventually the Americans with their heavily loaded wagons. Politically, the newcomers would prevail. But happily it was not to erase the old, but to learn good things from it. Anglos enjoy tortillas in Santa Fe.

Kozlowski's Spring was a dependable water source and often a campsite for Trail caravans.

The ancient Indian pueblo, or village, of Pecos was long the gateway to the plains, where nomadic Indians of the plains came to trade with the farming Pueblos. In early years of Santa Fe Trail traffic the village still was occupied—it was abandoned in 1838. The ruins of the old Pecos Mission are now part of Pecos National Historical Park, New Mexico.

"Zey foight six hour by my vatch, and my vatch vas slow!!"

Alexander Valle, 1866.

Originally the Trail was a route for America's westward expansion. But even after the country had expanded, and made the Trail an internal road, it remained important. When the United States came to deadly blows with itself in our own Civil War, opposing armies marched again on the Santa Fe Trail, finally colliding here at Pigeon's Ranch.

Pigeon's Ranch was a hostelry on the Santa Fe Trail, built the same year Fort Union was built. Here traders stopped for the night, used the good well, and sometimes traded livestock and stories with the owner, a man named Valle who was a retired trapper.

Shortly after the War Between the States broke out, Henry Sibley, in command at Fort Union, resigned his commission and went with the South. He proposed to the Confederacy that he would lead an invasion force up the old Camino Real from Texas to Santa Fe, then out the Santa Fe Trail and up to Denver to capture the gold and silver fields there. It's not clear what the rest of his plans were, nor if they had any chance of success. At any rate they ended here at Pigeon's Ranch in what came to be called the Battle of Glorieta Pass.

Word of the invasion electrified the Union men in the Colorado goldfields. Hurriedly organizing, they left Denver on February 22, 1862, and marched south to pick up the Santa Fe Trail just above Raton Pass. Going over the pass in a snowstorm, they got to Fort Union on March 10. They'd marched an incredible 400 miles in 13 days, mostly in terrible weather.

Barely pausing at the fort to pick up troops there, they continued on down the Trail, rounding the big "fishhook" bend by San Miguel and camping March 25 at Kozlowski's Spring, near the Pecos Ruins. There were preliminary brushes with the Confederates, approaching from the other end of the pass, and then the main encounter happened on the 28th. The two forces, entering the pass from opposite ends, met here at Pigeon's Ranch.

That the Union won was a fluke, in a way. Though the Confederates prevailed in the actual struggle in the pass, a Union detachment had circled behind them and managed to destroy the Confederate supply train, camped outside the pass at the Santa Fe end. You can win a battle but lose a war, and hungry, supply-less Confederates retreated to Texas.

And the slow "vatch"? That was old man Valle, describing the battle later. After the war he tried, but largely failed to get reimbursement from the federal government for the destruction of much of his hostelry, as he had to rebuild to get back into business on the Santa Fe Trail.

The Santa Fe Trail—a century later. The long curve of Interstate 25 along Rowe Mesa in New Mexico, nearing Santa Fe. The road (and railroad) roughly parallels the fading ruts of the old Trail. Travelers and cargo haulers still follow "the Trail", though the "wagons" are faster, the trip immeasurably easier.

The cabin at Pigeon's Ranch, Glorieta Pass, New Mexico, scene of the Battle of Glorieta Pass, March 1862. Union forces marching into the pass on the Santa Fe Trail (under the road in this photo— they came from the left) were filling canteens at this hostelry when they encountered the Confederates. The fluke northern victory secured New Mexico and Colorado to the Union.

"Los Americanos! Los carros! La entrada de la caravana!"

In 1984, an intrepid trio of hikers hiked the Santa Fe Trail—it took them three months. They camped the last night in this writer's backyard, a few miles short of Santa Fe, to finish their hike the next day and be given the keys to the city. One asked me what the glow in the sky was, and I told him, "Santa Fe." It shook him, and he commented on it the rest of the night: "You mean it's just there? Just over the hill?"

Surely it was ten times that in Trail days. We know from various journals that it was customary to stop a few miles out, put on a clean shirt if there was one for the occasion, cut each other's hair (until an entrepreneur set up shop out there to do it for them), and put fresh "poppers" on the awesome whips. Then they rounded the corner of the mountains and started down the long downslope, now paved but still called "Old Santa Fe Trail." Then citizens of Santa Fe who saw them coming called to each other, "Los Americanos! Los carros! La entrada de la caravana!"

The comments they wrote in their journals over the next few days contrasted with the obvious excitement of finishing the trek, of simply succeeding in getting here. Cultures rarely impress each other on first view, and Santa Fe was indeed a poor town. Easterners accustomed to wooden houses derided houses made of "mud"—though today an adobe (not mud) house in Santa Fe will set you back a small fortune. And Gregg, a more astute observer than most, did note that the thick walls kept the interior cool in summer and warm in winter.

That streets were dirt was no problem—they were in most towns in the East too. But the natives! They didn't look or sound like us. And women smoked! But how strongly the reader today wishes we had more journals to give the impressions of the folks who watched the wagons come in. One doubts that a teamster from the Missouri frontier, fresh off a prairie crossing, would win many prizes himself!

But whatever impression might come later, there was work to be done. The wagons worked their crowded, creaking way down the narrow streets and into the plaza in front of the Palace of the Governors, and did a noisy circuit in celebration. If it hadn't been taken care of by "express" riders coming ahead of the train, there was the necessary call at the palace for customs and duty payment. Then it was time to start unpacking into some rented storefront. The crossing was over. It was time to make a profit in Santa Fe.

After the long prairie crossing, traders came to civilization again in Santa Fe. Often first impressions were disdainful—in both directions—but a century later Americans flock to Santa Fe, a tourist mecca. There truly was something precious at the end of the Santa Fe Trail.

Interior of San Miguel Church, Santa Fe. Often called "the oldest church in the U.S.A.," this church was centuries old when the trade over the Trail opened.

"I can see the tired drivers at noonday lying under the shade of the wagons, their hats covering their faces.... I can see the tired sweaty mules rolling over and over in the grass delighted to be free from the heavy wagons."

Marian Russell, remembering at age 89.

Epilogue

Few wagons that actually crossed the Santa Fe Trail are left today. It is a disappointment to the modern student of the Trail, who would love to find one to see and touch, to know it actually lurched across Ash Creek one stormy afternoon. Still, there was not much reason to keep one. Even in the latter days of the Trail, when great wagons were custom-made for it, the crossing took its toll. Besides, much of the return trade did not require wagons. Wool did, but if instead of wool you'd traded for Mexican silver, or for a herd of mules to take back to sell in Missouri (the famous "Missouri mule" began life as a Santa Fe mule!), then it made more sense to sell the trail-worn vehicle for local use in Santa Fe.

But just how many wagons, or any of the goods that a wagon carried, could the little agricultural colony of Santa Fe absorb? Not much. Within just a few years after the opening of the Trail, those wagons had hauled in all the bottles and pans, the textiles and books and nails, that tiny Santa Fe could absorb. No matter. Santa Fe was just for starters. Soon wagons simply paused in Santa Fe as the entryway to Mexico, bargained with government officials about tax and tariff rates, and hitched up the teams again. Only now they rolled onto the immensely older Camino Real, the royal road to points south.

One may remember that in the 1700s, Santa Fe colonists, restricted by law to trading with Spanish merchants, had formed large, annual treks south to Chihuahua City. There, as customers everywhere without a choice, they usually found prices jacked sky-high for their one chance to shop. It may have seemed like justice to them, then, to see their own merchants' wagons as well as those of the American entrepreneurs, hauling away to the south to undercut the merchants there!

The wagons are gone. Farmers and local merchants bought the battered overland wagons to finish wearing them out in rough fields, and short trips to town on local roads. And when they got too bad, they could always be cannibalized for parts for the wagon that replaced them. Iron flanges that had held over torturous Raton Pass, and made a hundred trips to town after that, eventually broke—probably in iron-poor New Mexico a blacksmith worked them into

something else. A sideboard that had soaked in prairie storms and dried in prairie sun would be reused until it cracked beyond repair, to end as fire wood or the side of a pigpen.

Most of the cargo the great wagons hauled is gone now. Time wore out most of it, save for a few precious family heirlooms. No matter. The greater cargo was the social and commercial glue that brought two peoples together. The entire Southwest with its rich and delicious Spanish heritage that so improves our national stew, is the gift of the Santa Fe Trail to the United States.

It was a commercial, freight-hauling road. The keen-eyed professionals who crossed kept their attention on the bottom line. Transportation costs could eat profits. And yet, even in their day and not just by some modern romantic notion, the Santa Fe Trail turned out to be more than that. Journal after journal records the cost of goods, and the stream crossings, and the disaster of Indian attack. But in camp at night somewhere on the prairie, or maybe a final camp that came after the Trail was closed by the railroad, and old men remembered, that's not what they wrote about. Then they remembered the experience itself. Historian Marc Simmons spends hours with dusty ledgers, but he found this old poem too, and it may count for as much as the ledgers:

So, when the night has drawn its veil
The teams plod, span on span,
and one sees o'er the long dead trail
A ghostly caravan.

SUGGESTED READING

GREGG, JOSIAH. *Commerce of the Prairie.* Lincoln: University of Nebraska Press, 1967.

MAGOFFIN, SUSAN. *Down the Santa Fe Trail and Into Mexico.* Lincoln: University of Nebraska Press, 1982.

SIMMONS, MARC. *Following the Santa Fe Trail.* Santa Fe, New Mexico: Ancient City Press, 1986.

Preceding Pages: Trail ruts near Fort Union, New Mexico.

Books in the "Voyage of Discovery" series: California Trail, Lewis & Clark, Mormon Trail, Oregon Trail, John Wesley Powell, Santa Fe Trail. Also available is a book on the Oregon Trail Center near Baker City, Oregon.
Selected titles in this series can be ordered with a booklet in German or Spanish bound into the center of the English book.
Call (800-626-9673), fax (702-433-3420), or write to the address below.

Published by KC Publications, 3245 E. Patrick Ln., Suite A, Las Vegas, NV 89120.

Created, Designed, and Published in the U.S.A.
Printed by Doosan Dong-A Co., Ltd., Seoul, Korea
Paper produced exclusively by Hankuk Paper Mfg. Co., Ltd.